C000183121

Victorian and Edwardian Glasgow from old photographs

Maurice Lindsay

Victorian and Edwardian Glasgow from old photographs

B. T. Batsford Ltd · London

First published 1987

ISBN 0 7134 5302 8 (cased)

Printed in Great Britain by
Butler & Tanner Limited
Frome and London
for the publishers
B T Batsford Limited
4 Fitzhardinge Street
London
W1H 0AH

Acknowledgements

Some of these photographs came to light as a result of forays into the collections held by Strathclyde Regional Archive; in particular nos 27, 32, 40, 41, 42, 58, 89, 100, 101, 102, 105 and 108.

While others came to my notice through the Strathclyde Archive files and indexes, better prints subsequently turned up in the collections of The Mitchell Library, Glasgow; to Mr Joe Fisher and his staff in the Glasgow Room I am in many ways indebted. I have taken from the Graham, Young and miscellaneous collections there, and from The Mitchell Library copies of Annan publications nos 1, 2, 3, 4, 5, 6, 7, 8, 9, 10, 11, 12, 13, 14, 15, 16, 17, 18, 19, 20, 21, 22, 23, 24, 25, 28, 29, 30, 31, 33, 34, 35, 36, 37, 38, 39, 43, 44, 45, 46, 47, 48, 49, 50, 51, 52, 53, 54, 55, 59, 60, 61, 62, 63, 64, 65, 66, 68, 69, 70, 71, 72, 73, 74, 75, 76, 77, 78, 79, 80, 81, 82, 83, 84, 85, 87, 88, 90, 91, 92, 93, 94, 95, 103, 104, 106, 107, 109, 110, 111, 112, 113, 114, 115, 116, 117 and 118.

To Messrs. Thomas Annan & Sons I am indebted directly for copies of nos 67 and 86 and to Mr Hamish Swan, Chairman and Managing Director of Tennant Caledonian Breweries Ltd for nos 98 and 99.

Mr David Bruce kindly read my essay on Glasgow photographers and made several helpful suggestions. My secretary, Mrs Doris Cairns, always willingly, made various enquiries on my behalf and typed the manuscript, while my wife most helpfully corrected the proofs.

1

There have been several Glasgows. The Romans moved around the Clyde, but their Antonine wall, the west end of which began at Bowling, veered east, running north of the future city. The first Glasgow was therefore the mediaeval village by a crossroads, near a shallow ford on the river Clyde much used by travellers journeying between the Western Highlands and the Lowlands. It possessed a monastery church dedicated to St Mungo, built in the year 543. This was replaced in 1136 by the first cathedral, also named after the patron saint of the place. Mungo came to Glasgow as a young monk, bearing the body of his teacher, Fergus, on a cart drawn by two bulls. According to legend, where the bulls stopped, Mungo was to bury Fergus and set up his monastery. This he did. He, in his turn, was eventually also buried there. Today, his tomb may be seen in the lower church of the present cathedral.

The first cathedral burned down in 1190. A new cathedral was re-consecrated in 1197. Part of the south-western section of the lower church and sections of the lower walls of the nave may have been erected by Bishop Jocelin's twelfth-century masons for the first cathedral; but the Glasgow Cathedral we have today is substantially the outcome of Bishop William de Bondington's re-building between 1233 and 1258. It employs the form of early Gothic known in Scotland as First Pointed and has a nave and eight bays, a central tower and transept and a choir of five bays with eastern chapels beyond. Beneath the choir is the lower church, with the chapter house in the north-east angle. The west front of the nave was originally flanked by two towers of differing size and character. These were taken down in 1846, one being unsafe and both thought by some to disfigure the façade. Although, soon after, money was raised to replace them, the cathedral has been left ever since with its present rather shorn appearance.

Glasgow was granted a charter by William the Lion around 1175, and about 1190 granted the right to hold an Annual Fair.

An important development was the 'bryg', or bridge, of five stone arches, put up in 1345 to replace the wooden one at the Stockwell Shallows. This Old Glasgow Bridge did duty until 1847, being replaced in 1854 by the present Stockwell Bridge. Glasgow's increasing importance was further confirmed in 1451 when Bishop William Turnbull founded the second Scottish university (St Andrew's University had been founded in 1413) on a site in Rottenrow.

The earliest Glasgow street pattern took the form of a cross, twice repeated. At the top of the town – largely cleared of buildings since the Second World War, its former associations commemorated today by the Townhead roundabout – were the Cathedral and the Bishop's Palace, which stood just above the Mollindinar Burn, a tributary of the Clyde now almost totally covered over. The houses to the south and along the upper cross belonged to the clergy. The Hiegait, now the High Street, curved down to the Merchant Town, centred on Glasgow Cross. To the east ran the Gallow Gait, where the city's gallows stood. Westward from the Cross was St Thenew's Gait – called after St Mungo's mother, whose name is still commemorated in the corrupted form of St Enoch. The north-to-south road

THE POST OFFICE DIRECTORY,
BY JOSEPH SWAN.
65 St Vincent Street
LANDS OF HAMILTONHILL
CRAIGBANK
CRAIGHALL
NORTHPARK
WOODLANDS
KELVIN-GROVE
KELVINBANK
LANDS OF STOBCROSS
LANDS OF OVERNEWTON
THE HARBOUR OF GLASGOW
RAILWAY DEPOT
PLANTATION
ARGYLL STREET
BROOMIELAW
SAUCHIEHALL
ST VINCENT
WEST GEORGE
CRANSTONHILL
THE RIVER KELVIN

LANDS OF PETERSHILL
ROSEBANK
TRACK OF THE GARNKIRK AND GLASGOW RAILWAY
CALEDONIAN RAILWAY
CHARLES STREET
MONKLAND
LANDS OF
CRAIGPARK
GOLFHILL
WHITEHILL
HOUSE OF REFUGE
Mill Dam
CAMLACHIE
DUKE STREET
TRONGATE
CLYDE STREET
EAST CLYDE ST
GLASGOW GREEN
THE RIVER CLYDE
KINGS PARK
FLESHERS HAUCH
HUTCHESONTOWN
GORBALS
HAYFIELD STREET
SOUTHERN NECROPOLIS
CALEDONIAN
CUMBERLAND
CAVENDISH ST.
BRIDGETON
CALTON
CATTLE MARKET
BARRACKS FOR INFANTRY
Garbals Burying Ground

was the Walker Gait, street of the fullers who beat cloth to cleanse and thicken it; this is now the Saltmarket. Where the Mollindinar curved west to meet the Clyde, a bridge was built in the thirteenth century. This continuation was known as the Briggait or Bridge Gait. Several lateral streets completed the 'grid-iron pattern', as it came to be called when it was repeated and expanded in later years.

As the mediaeval city grew, it changed its legal status, becoming first a Burgh of Regality in 1450, the Bishop representing the King's authority rather than, as formerly, ruling in his own right. In 1690, Glasgow achieved the status of a Royal Burgh, being then directly answerable only to Parliament and the King.

The city's developing trade links were marked by the recognition in 1605 of both its Trades House and its Merchants House. Around their activities a new middle class came into being, the merchants being the exporters and importers, wealthier than the craftsmen and shopkeepers. The members of these two corporations gradually took over the running of the City from the Church, and for more than 250 years effectively controlled the Town Council.

The second Glasgow was created out of the wealth earned after the Union of Parliaments in 1707. This enabled the Scots to trade abroad more freely, and led to the build-up of the commercial empire of the Tobacco Lords. Apparently as a result of the French war, which made the Atlantic off the south-west English coast dangerous to shipping, Glasgow developed into the main port receiving tobacco from the Colonies of Virginia, North Carolina and Maryland, subsequently exporting much of it to France and the Low Countries.

The names of some of the men who dominated this trade live on in modern Glasgow. Andrew Cochrane, Lord Provost of the city when Bonny Prince Charlie took it over during his southward march in 1745, attributed the upsurge of Glasgow's prosperity to the success of four young men: Alexander Spiers of Elderslie, James Ritchie of Busby, William Cunningham of Lainshaw and John Glassford of Dougalston. All built great mansions for themselves, surrounded by large gardens. Only Cunningham's mansion survives, off Buchanan Street, converted, first, into the Royal Exchange by the addition of David Hamilton's massive Corinthian pillars and entablature between 1827–29, and in our own day, re-adapted internally to house Stirling's Library, the bequest of a Victorian Glaswegian. Glassford was a shipowner as well as a tobacco trader. He had the misfortune to find himself at the end of his life in financial difficulties, a terrible crime in later Victorian eyes. Nevertheless, they still named a street after him.

The Colonies badly needed manufactured goods, and Glasgow was in a position to manufacture and supply them. The City's industrial base was thus founded upon the demand for things which could be exported to the Colonies in the ships that brought in the tobacco.

The Glasgow of the Tobacco Lords, surrounded by fields and trees, still seemed to manage to contain its industries without suffering much obvious environmental damage. Architecturally too, being new, it was presumably 'all of a piece'. It certainly won the praise of Daniel Defoe early in the eighteenth century, encomiums from the novelist Tobias Smollett in the middle of the century and enthusiasm from Dorothy Wordsworth as late as 1772. The well-contained urban industry in a city the population of which was 43,000 in 1780 was vividly celebrated in a poem written by John Mayne, a Dumfriesshire disciple of Burns, in 1783:

> In ilka house, frae man to boy,
> A' hands in Glasgow find employ;
> Even little maids, wi' meikle joy,
>   Flower lawn and gauze,
> Or clip wi' care the silken soy
>   For ladies' braws . . .
>
> Look through the town! The houses here
> Like noble palaces appear;
> A' things the face o' gladness wear
>   The market's thrang,
> Business is brisk, and a's asteer
>   The streets alang.

Clean-keepit streets! So lang and braid,
The distant objects seem to fade;
And then for shelter or for shade
  Frae sun or shower,
Piazzas lend their friendly aid
  At ony hour ...

Wondering, we see new streets extending,
New squares wi' public buildings blending,
Brigs, stately brigs, in arches bending
  Across the Clyde,
And turrets, kirks and spires ascending
  In lofty pride ...

Wow, sirs! Its wonderfu' to trace
How Commerce has improved the place.
Changing bare house-room's narrow space,
  And want o' money
To seats o' elegance and grace,
  And milk and honey.

In 1775, the American War of Independence abruptly ended the tobacco trade and in 1793 the Napoleonic Wars similarly affected the parallel trade in rum and sugar with Jamaica. With these reverses, many an eighteenth-century fortune vanished. Three Glasgow banks – the Arms, the Merchants' and Thompson's – all closed their doors during 1793, while the Thistle Bank only just survived. Only the Ships Bank, run by a dour and canny Glaswegian, Robert Carrick, managed to weather the general collapse.

By then, however, other Glasgow entrepreneurs had set about manufacturing with fresh energy, at first using machines imported from England, Holland or France. By 1805, David Macpherson could write in his *Annals of Commerce*:

Before America became independent of Great Britain, the foreign commerce of Glasgow was chiefly with that country; and consequently it was deranged by that event. But the enterprising spirit of the merchants has found new channels of commerce, sufficient to employ their capitals and industry. They have also turned their attention more than formerly to manufactures, whereby the city has become the centre and fostering parent of a prodigious number of manufacturing establishments. They have thirty print fields within the influence of this hive of industry. The towns and villages in a circuit of many miles around, and some at considerable distances, are filled with spinners, weavers, and many other classes of work-people, depending upon the fabrics of the loom and the stocking frames; there are in the neighbourhood several iron-works for making cannon and all other articles of cast iron, which, taken collectively are perhaps scarcely inferior to the Carron Works.[1] The works for window glass, bottle glass and ornamental glass are extensive and thriving. Sugar baking, malting and brewing are all established concerns. But it would be almost as difficult to particularise all the manufactures of Glasgow as those of London, and it may suffice to say that manufactures of almost every kind are carried on with spirit and activity, and generally in joint stocks by companies, or, as they are generally called here, *concerns*, under management of one or more of the partners; and that the manufactures requiring fire have the vast advantage of coals close to the city.

The third Glasgow – the Glasgow of Victorian and Edwardian days – thus emerged out of the fall of the second. It was enabled to do so largely because of the invention of a method of perfecting the harnessing of steam. The solution to this problem came to a Greenock-born instrument-maker in Glasgow University while he was walking across Glasgow Green one Sunday afternoon in 1746. James Watt recorded that he was thinking about the steam engine at the time 'when the idea came into my mind that as steam was an elastic body, it would rush into a vacuum, and if a communication was made between the cylinder and exhausted vessel, it would rush into it, and might there be condensed without cooling the cylinder ... I had not walked further than the golf-house when the whole thing was arranged in my mind.'

The steam engine, applied to Hargreaves's spinning jenny and Arkwright's spinning frame, led to the mechanization of cotton products and eventually to the elimination of the handloom weavers who flourished in and around Glasgow.

But other processes were quickly established. J. N. R. Tennent had been brewing at Wellpark in Glasgow, since 1785. The St Rollox Chemical Works had been founded in 1800 by unrelated Charles Tennant – Burns's 'Wabster Charlie' – to produce a bleaching agent which was to gain European supremacy. Charles Mackintosh, a dyestuffs manufacturer, set up a Glasgow factory to produce rainproof 'Mackintoshes' in 1834. Black band ironstone had been discovered in the west of Scotland by David Mushet in 1801. In 1828, J. B. Neilson discovered how to use hot instead of cold air in the blasting furnace. The combination of hot-blast furnace and black band ironstone produced the recipe for cheap pig iron, which cut coal consumption in its manufacture by at least 50 per cent. In 1830, Glasgow had 25 furnaces; by 1843 there were 62.

The arrival of the railway for organized passenger traffic – as opposed to earlier coal traffic lines – came with the opening of the Glasgow and Garnkirk railway in 1827. Ten years later Paisley, Kilmarnock and Ayr were linked to Glasgow by rail. By 1842, Glasgow and Edinburgh had a rail link, and by 1848 it was possible to reach London by rail.

Shipbuilding, heavy engineering and the production of chemicals and a wide range of manufactured goods led to a further rapid expansion of the city. In 1801 the population was 77,000, by 1821 147,000 and by 1861 448,000, although by then Glasgow had begun to 'acquire' its earlier suburbs, subsequently incorporating them within the city boundaries. Cheap labour to man all this industrial expansion came from the Highlands and, especially around the time of the Irish potato famine of 1846, from across the Irish Sea. What survived of the mediaeval heart of Glasgow was soon grossly overcrowded and disease-ridden, once-proud houses quickly descending to the condition of slums.

Many of the men who fashioned Glasgow's industrial revolution established their houses outside the city. Some built fine country mansions in estates on the outskirts, like Garscadden or Kelvin House. Almost all of these houses of 'The Old Gentry' have long since been destroyed to make way for the expanding city. Other leaders of industry and commerce lived in the new residential Glasgow, begun during the closing years of the eighteenth century. George Square was designed about 1782, though today only the North British Hotel (now the Copthorne), adjacent to Queen Street Station, survives from Georgian times. Robert Adam's Trades House went up in 1794 and still graces Ingram Street, though his New Assembly Rooms unfortunately made way for the General Post Office as the twentieth century came in. John Brash's Blythswood Square – at the top of what was once known as Harley's Hill after its promoter, William Harley, a pioneer in introducing piped water to the City, and who planned an elegant Vauxhall-style pleasure garden for his hilltop – was built around 1823.

In a similar style, if perhaps rather less elegant, Glasgow's classical 'new town' soon filled out Bath Street, Regent Street, West George Street and the other grid-iron pattern streets which soon crossed all sides of the hill. Blythswood Square, now marred by a hideously replaced corner-stop building put up during the 1950s, is one of Glasgow's outstanding Conservation Areas. Even by the late 1850s, however, the 'new town' streets were experiencing the intrusion of commerce and the replacement of individual buildings by much larger Victorian ones. Today, many of these same Victorian buildings, excellent in their own right but out of scale with the Blythswood-style originals, are being replaced by twentieth-century edifices, about most of which comment in this context would be as inappropriate as it might be contentious.

Detached villages, like the Gorbals and Govan on the south side of the Clyde, like Partick to the west – thought in the 1870s likely to be developed as the 'workshop' of the West End – and like Springburn to the north, were first of all physically caught up in the expanding city and then, inevitably, in the interest of good administration, absorbed by it.

By the time the American Civil War led to the ending of Glasgow's supremacy in the cotton trade, it was often being claimed that almost every article used in other parts of the world was manufactured in Glasgow. Clydeside shipyards pioneered the wooden steamship, the iron ship and the steel-hulled ship. Attempts to produce steel had begun as early as 1857, but it was not until the 1880s that the great steel foundries came fully into production. By 1900, there were 150 open-hearth furnaces in and around Glasgow, producing around 605,000 tons of steel in various forms.

The poet Alexander Smith's 'Glasgow' catches the throbbing momentum of the City at that time:

Draw thy fierce streams of blinding ore,
Smite on a thousand anvils, roar
  Down to the harbour-bars;
Smoulder in smoky sunsets, flare
On rainy nights, when street and square
  Lie empty to the stars.
From terrace proud to alley base
I know thee as my mother's face.

When sunset bathes thee in his gold,
In wreathes of bronze thy sides are rolled,
  Thy smoke is dusky fire;
And, from the glory round thee poured,
A sunbeam like an angel's sword
  Shivers upon a spire.
Thus have I watched thee, Terror! Dream!
When the blue Night crept up the stream.

The wild train plunges in the hills,
He shrieks across the midnight rills;
  Streams through the shifting glare,
The roar and flap of foundry fires,
That shake with light the sleeping shires;
  And on the moorlands bare,
He sees afar a crown of light
Hang o'er thee in the hollow night.

At midnight, when thy suburbs lie
As silent as a noonday sky,
  When larks with heat are mute,
I love to linger on thy bridge,
All lonely as a mountain ridge,
  Disturbed but by my foot;
While the black lazy stream beneath
  Steals from its far-off wilds of heath.

And through thy heart, as through a dream,
Flows on that black disdainful stream;
  All scornfully it flows,
Between the huddled gloom of masts,
Silent as pines unvexed by blasts –
  'Tween lamps in streaming rows.
O wondrous sight! O stream of dread!
O long dark river of the dead!...

Many of the early passenger liners owned by such famous shipping concerns as Cunard – the deed of partnership of which, incidentally, had been drawn up by John Park Fleming, a Glasgow lawyer whose family became residential developers in the City – White Star and the City Line came from Clydeside yards; among them, in 1910, was the *Lusitania*, taker of the Blue Riband from a German rival. Sunk by a German torpedo during the First World War, the *Lusitania*'s record for an Atlantic crossing had been four days, ten hours and 40 minutes: a far cry from the eighteen days taken by the early Clyde-built Cunarder *Syrius* in 1838.

One of the benefits a thriving shipbuilding industry bestows on a locality is that it gives rise to the development of a wide range of ancillary trades, all of which increase prosperity. Glasgow celebrated that prosperity by mounting a series of great exhibitions in 1888, 1901, 1911 and – a final brave flourish in the face of gathering adversity – 1938. The 1888 Exhibition, the biggest and best hitherto held outside London, was laid out in the Kelvingrove Park. The main pavilion was constructed on what is now the site of the Kelvingrove Art Galleries, itself designed for the 1911 Exhibition. Oriental in character, the 1888 Exhibition was nicknamed 'Baghdad on the Kelvin' by Glaswegians. Almost six million people passed through its turnstiles. The 1901 Exhibition, nicknamed 'The Groveries', was intended to illustrate the growth of art, industry and science during the nineteenth century and was actually the largest exhibition to have been held anywhere in Britain at that time. It drew 11½ million visitors, one of its main attractions being the Machinery Hall, which stood on the site of today's Kelvin Hall. The 1911 Exhibition, planned during the Edwardian period, was officially named the Scottish Exhibition of History, Art, and Industry, and had as one of its objects the endowment of a Chair of Scottish History and Literature at Glasgow University. One of its features was an 'old-world Scottish toonie'. Another was a pavilion of Old Glasgow. The main pavilion was modelled on Falkland Palace. Almost 9½ million people attended, enthralled, no doubt, by the flotilla of model ships floating about on the Kelvin.

All three Exhibitions enjoyed fine weather, unlike the 1938 Exhibition, which experienced one of the wettest Scottish summers of the twentieth century. Its very existence, however, underlined the curious fact that many aspects of Edwardian, even Victorian Glasgow, survived into the 'twenties and the 'thirties; and so, at one remove, came into my own boyhood experience. Indeed, it was only after the 1939–45 War that the reaction against the supposed stability of Victorianism fully set in.

The result, environmentally, during the next 25 or so years was the sweeping away of much that was shoddy or rendered purposeless because of changing technology. With the destruction of the jerry-built and the obsolete, unfortunately, also went that of many fine buildings which the more enlightened policy of conservation which gradually prevailed after the passing of the Civic Amenities Act of 1967 (subsequently incorporated in both Scottish and English planning law) would have sought to have adapted for new uses. Happily, however, much of the best survived the insensitivity of the early planners,[2] the stupidity of unimaginative elected representatives and the cupidity of developers.

2

The fabric of Glasgow has undergone change in response to differing economic developments. Glasgow Cathedral and Provand's Lordship, originally St Nicholas Hospital, are the only buildings that survive from mediaeval Glasgow. Little more has come down to us from the beautiful and often-praised Glasgow of Georgian times. The present Tron Kirk building, now a theatre, went up on the site of the Collegiate Church of the Blessed St Mary, destroyed by fire in 1793. Only the seventeenth-century steeple of the Tollbooth or town house still stands, the main building being demolished in 1921. Another building that clings on by the steeple, so to say, is that of the old Merchants' House, built, perhaps, by Sir William Bruce for Campbell of Blytheswood, and now a centrepiece of the modern Briggait development. The interior of the old hall was built into the new Merchant House, which went up in George Square in 1874–7 (the upper storeys were added in 1907/8).

The noblest entire relic of the Glasgow of the old Tobacco Lords is thus Alan Dreghorn's St Andrews Church, off the Saltmarket, begun in 1739 and 17 years in the building. All that survives of the Old College is the reconstructed façade on the Pearce Lodge at Gilmorehill.

The fabric of mediaeval and Georgian Glasgow simply could not stand up to the expansionary pressures of the city's nineteenth-century industrial development. The long gardens of once-noble houses were rapidly filled with shoddy tenements. Such was the appalling overcrowding at the heart of the city after the Irish influx of the 1840s that the Town Council decided to acquire the properties in the mediaeval centre of the city and demolish them, replacing them with modern tenements. Permission to do this was secured with the passing of the City of Glasgow Improvement Act in 1866. Six acres, spread over seven separate areas, were demolished and rebuilt under the powers granted by the Act. Once it had been passed, the City fathers tore down 'backlands', wynds, courts and closes, some of which had once been fine old houses, in the High Street, Saltmarket and the Gallowgate, or picturesque thatched dwellings in the village-like main street of Gorbals. The process of destruction accelerated when the railway companies swathed through the handsome seventeenth-century Merchants' Houses in the Briggait to bring in their lines. The City Improvement Trust, through whom the Town Council operated, had, in fact, no other weapon at their disposal with which to combat the disease and human misery brought about by overcrowding and grossly unhygienic conditions. In 1839, the author of a Parliamentary Report on Housing in Great Britain recorded:

> I have seen human degradation in some of the worst places, both in England and abroad, but I did not believe until I had visited the wynds of Glasgow that so large an amount of filth, crime, misery and disease existed in one spot in any civilised country.

The authors of a report of 1842 on *The Sanitary Conditions of the Labouring Population* stated:

> It appeared to us that both the structural arrangements and the conditions of the population in Glasgow were the worst of any we had seen in any part of Great Britain. In the courts

> of Argyle Street there were no privies or drains, and the dung heaps received all the filth which the swarms of wretched inhabitants could give. We learned that a considerable part of the rents for the houses was paid by the produce of these dung heaps ... The picture is so shocking that without ocular proof one would be disposed to doubt the possibility of the facts ... Several women were found lying in a house under a blanket while others were then out of doors wearing all the articles of dress belonging to the party.

The first Medical Officer of Health, William (later Sir William) Gairdner, was not appointed until 1863. In spite of the improving measures which he and his successors gradually managed to have imposed, insanitary conditions persisted and were to remain a threat for several more decades.

Unfortunately, the University was persuaded to move, the professors understandably disliking their insanitary neighbourhood. The Old College, with its three Courts, likened by some to a mediaeval Oxford college, was torn down to make way for a railway goods yard, undoubtedly the most grievous architectural loss Glasgow has so far suffered. The professors left their mediaeval heritage in 1870, to move into a new neo-Gothic University, built for them out west, on Gilmorehill, by Sir George Gilbert Scott, the designer of London's Albert Memorial.

During the 1830s, '40s and '50s, Charles Wilson and others were adorning Woodlands Hill with its crowning circus and those crescents and terraces on the slope that today constitute another of Glasgow's Outstanding Conservation Areas. The Park Conservation Area is dominated by the Italianate campanile of Wilson's Trinity College of 1856, now converted to office and domestic use. While this was going on, the westward expansion pushed across the Kelvin, into Kelvinside.

During the eighteenth century, Kelvinside was a rural estate owned by the Dunmoores, a Glasgow merchant family. It was let off in small farms. The Dunmoores' mansion of 1760, first known as Bankhead, later Kelvinside House, stood above the Kelvin surrounded by thick woodlands. A retired Nabob from Bengal, Thomas Lithan, bought the estate in 1785. His widow married a Glasgow lawyer and land speculator, Thomas Cuthill. He made no attempt to develop Kelvinside, but following Mrs Cuthill's death the estate was bought by a partnership made up of Matthew Montgomery, the senior partner in a Glasgow law firm, his own junior partner in the practice, John Park Fleming and the patentee of the 'hot blast' process in iron smelting, J. B. Neilson. Neilson soon withdrew from the arrangement, but the other two set about the development of Kelvinside as an area of good-quality middle-class housing. Until shortly before their purchase the estate was not linked to the city by a road. An Act of 1838 permitted the construction of a turnpike. By 1839 a road ran from Anniesland to the centre of the city.

The architect of London's Regent's Park and Calverley Park, near Tunbridge Wells, Decimus Burton, was called in to lay out the estate in 1846. Burton's plan was revised in 1858 by the architect James Salmon, who had by then already designed the East Glasgow suburb of Dennistoun.

High Windsor, now Kirklee Terrace, the first of the great terraces to go up along Great Western Road and still then in the country, was erected by Charles Wilson in 1845. Individual houses cost £2300 each. Kew Terrace was built between 1850 and 1853. J.T. Rochead's Grosvenor Terrace, with its Venetian fenestration, followed in 1855. It features in Guy McCrone's delightful trilogy of Glasgow novels, *Wax Fruit*. Then came Belhaven Terrace, East and West, and most notably, in 1870, Alexander 'Greek' Thomson's magnificent palace-like block, Great Western Terrace. By now, Glasgow was at the peak of its industrial affluence, and the pace of the development of Kelvinside and the areas adjacent increased.

I have devoted some space to Kelvinside for several reasons. Firstly, there is its undoubted architectural distinction. There is also its Botanic Gardens, opened in 1841 to subscribers of a guinea each, and for several decades the only garden of its kind outside London's Kew. Kelvinside's history has been well documented. We have full records, for example, of its transport arrangements; of the first horse-bus service of 1847, running from Cleveden Road to the centre of the city every two hours; of the horse-tram service, which took over in 1872 and provided a service until 1894, latterly under licence to Glasgow Corporation, and on to 1894, when the Corporation began running the service themselves. The electric tram appeared on Great Western Road in 1901.

Above all, Kelvinside has been well photographed. When the original members of the Kelvinside partnership died, just before the estate began to flourish, its affairs came into the hands of Montgomery's two surviving daughters, who lived in Moffat; but it was really the other two trustees, D.K. Fleming and James Brown Fleming, who together carried on their uncle's and father's partnership. By 1880, management was virtually in the sole hands of J.B. Fleming (1840–1899), a public figure well known as 'a dynamic extrovert with a sharp wit', who served on several public bodies, including the Glasgow Exchange. Less flatteringly, he was described by *The Bailie* magazine – the *Private Eye* of the 1870s and '80s – as being 'capacious of person, fiery of countenance and unconventional of manner'. In 1894, J.B. Fleming published a book of fine photographs of Kelvinside, prefacing his anthology with a revealing photograph of himself. As was the custom of the times no credit was given to the photographers. It has been suggested that some of these splendid studies may have been the work of Thomas Annan, or of his son John Craig Annan, but no evidence supports either attribution. In any case, Fleming was most certainly the entrepreneur responsible for providing us with a notable record of the Great Western Road terraces in their heyday.

The next major middle-class development occurred in the south. Sir John Maxwell of Pollok, the eighth baronet, began to feu off parts of his large estate, mostly for the construction of individual villas, although some tenements were allowed at the northern edge of it. He died before the development had progressed very far. The heir, his sister's son, Sir John Stirling-Maxwell, inherited Pollok in 1878, and continued to exercise the same strict quality control over its development that the previous Laird had insisted upon. Most of the area was taken up with handsome free-standing ashlar villas set in large gardens. Such a spacious development did not lend itself to collective photography, and only one early view is included here. Pollokshields is also now an Outstanding Conservation Area, though nearly all the mansions are divided into two or more flats.

By Edwardian times, Glasgow's local grey sandstone – much of it really honey-coloured, as we have rediscovered since it has been cleaned in our own time, freeing it from the pre-smokeless-zone accretion of domestic and industrial grime – ran out, and was replaced by red sandstone from Dumfries or the island of Arran. This continued to be used until 1939, when it gave place after the War to concrete (surely the most unsympathetic of all building materials) and, more recently, brick.

Just as the introduction of the American Otis's invention, the elevator, or lift, to Scotland in the 1850s enabled office buildings to carry more floors, so the introduction of the electric tramcar in 1890 increased the range and mobility of workers, although to some extent they had already been partially freed from the need to live within walking distance of their place of employment with the coming of the suburban railway.

The ability of their employers to enjoy the pleasures of the seaside developed quickly in the decades following the successful first crossing from Greenock to Helensburgh in 1812 of the first practical steamboat, the paddle steamer *Comet*. As paddle steamers became larger, more reliable and faster, villages like Dunoon were enlarged into residential towns, while whole new Victorian settlements grew up around clachans on the banks of the Firth and round the shores of its lochs. For those not so fortunate to be able to live in their own summer house and travel daily to work during July and August, an outing 'doon the watter' to Dunoon, Largs or Rothesay was the accepted way of spending the annual July Glasgow Fair holiday.

By 1901, when Queen Victoria died and King Edward came to the throne, Glasgow's population had risen to 762,000. By the census year

1911, just after King Edward's death, it had reached 784,455. Outside the time-span covered by this book, the population was to reach 1,300,000 during the 1930s, overtaking Birmingham and making Glasgow the 'second city of the Empire'. Today, its heavy industries and shipbuilding gone, this 'finest Victorian city in Britain', as the late Sir John Betjeman called it, is still contracting and, necessarily, changing its mode of life. We are not concerned here with these changes; but it should at least be recorded that, after suffering many misfortunes and making some dreadful mistakes, some in concrete and only too permanently visible, Glasgow seems now to have learned to conserve what is left of its stone and mortar heritage.

3

Until the 1840s, public events had to be illustrated either through 'action' drawings, such as the artists employed by the *Illustrated London News* excelled in, or, where an event was of sufficient historic significance, by painters, usually working from sketches. Many such drawings, etchings and paintings of Glasgow life have survived from the pre-photographic era.

Photography was invented, for practical purposes, simultaneously in England and France at the beginning of 1839, by William Henry Fox Talbot, an English landowner, and Louis J. M. Daguerre respectively. Talbot's paper negative/positive process was the one used with tremendous success by the Scottish partnership of David Octavius Hill and Robert Adamson during the 1840s, but it was probably the rival Daguerreotype, with its single silver-toned positive on metal, that produced the first photographs to be made in Scotland. Both systems were adopted in Scotland remarkably quickly, assisted by the fact, no doubt, that there were discrepancies in Scottish and English patent coverage, to the advantage of Scottish photographers. By 1842 at least one Daguerreotypist, Edwards, was operating in Glasgow, opening the City's first photographic studio, in Buchanan Street. We do not even know this enterprising Mr Edwards's first name, but a year later he appears also to have been operating in Dumfriesshire, and perhaps in other Scottish towns, mostly concerning himself with producing portraits costing one guinea each, 'including a handsome case or frame'.

It is likely that the first serious landscape photographer to operate in Scotland was Talbot, who arrived in 1844 to produce images for the second of his Calotype published albums, *Sun Pictures in Scotland*. It was the influence of Sir Walter Scott's poem *The Lady of the Lake* that took him to the Trossachs and Loch Katrine, where he sailed on the steamer *Rob Roy*.[3] The same influence, incidentally, led Thomas Cook to bring his first organized party of tourists from Leicester to Loch Katrine in 1846.[4]

A major advance was made with the introduction of the Collodion, or 'wet plate' process, invented in 1851 by Frederick Scott Archer. The negatives were made from a solution of guncotton dissolved in ether – extremely lethal, incidentally – and poured on to glass plates. The drawback to Collodion plates, apart from the fragility of the glass, was the weight of the stock which had to be carried around by the photographer. As the first roll film was not invented until 1885 (by the American George Eastman of Rochester, New York who in 1888 also produced and marketed the first portable roll camera, the Kodak No. 1 – 'YOU PRESS THE BUTTON: WE DO THE REST' was the advertising slogan), much of the heritage of Scottish photography from the mid-Victorian years was captured by the wet plate method, though many early Calotypes, in a purply sepia, do survive.

The most famous of Scotland's native early photographers, the painter David Octavius Hill, with his associate Robert Adamson, operated mainly in Edinburgh from their Rock House studio on the Calton Hill, for the most part contenting themselves with Edinburgh and east coast subjects. In the late 1840s, before he succumbed to the quick rewards of commercialism, George Washington Wilson produced good work in Aberdeen as did Thomas Keith in Edinburgh and James Valentine of Dundee. Though he worked for a time in Portugal, the country of his birth, another early photographer, Duncan Brown, did leave some impressions of Clydeside life, though unfortunately, many of his images have faded badly. Other early Scottish photographers include W. D. Clarke and Archibald Burns. The three dimensional stereoscope photograph, perfected by Sir David Brewster, caught Victorian fancy. Stereoscopic views were bought in packets. Much of the Scottish demand for commercial views of this sort was satisfied from the Aberdeen studio of Washington Wilson and the Dundee studio of James Valentine, both ultimately made famous and prosperous by their production of postcards.

The most celebrated of Glasgow's early photographers was undoubtedly Thomas Annan (1830–1888), a friend of Hill. Annan was the fifth of the seven children of a flax spinner and miller at Dairsie, Fife. Much to his father's annoyance, young Thomas had himself apprenticed to a Linlithgow lithographer. Annan set up his first studio in Woodlands Cottage, Woodlands Road, where he announced himself as being a Calotype Printer, a definition that has puzzled some photographic historians, since by 1855, the Collodion process had superseded Calotypes; but it probably simply meant that he made paper, not metal, photographs. In 1857, Annan moved his studio to 116 Sauchiehall Street and in 1859 to 202 Hope Street. Much of his early bread-and-butter work consisted of photographing the paintings owned by rich Glaswegians. He was joined in the photographic business by his brother, Robert, in 1873.

It was the Trustees of the Glasgow Improvements Scheme who commissioned Annan to take pictures of the closes and wynds and narrow passages soon to be torn down to make way for new buildings on a site of 88 acres. Between 1868 and 1871 Annan took 31 photographs. The wet Collodion process was used, although the printing was done on albumen paper, which had an unfortunate tendency to fade. Some sets of these albumen prints were bound together; according to Anita Ventura Mosley, two sets;[5] according to the expert on the subject, J. A. Fisher of Glasgow's Mitchell Library, fourteen sets.[6] There was a depression in 1877, bringing the Trust's operations to a standstill that was to last for a decade.

In May of that year the Trustees of the Improvements Act were asked to provide a set of photographs of 'various old and historical parts of Glasgow as existing previous to the commencement of the operations of the Trust; for exhibition at the Kelvingrove Park Museum'. At the same time several members of the Trust asked that they might have copies of the photographs. The Trustees therefore agreed to provide albums for each member. The architect to the Trust, John Carrick, was instructed 'to prepare the accompanying introductory and descriptive letterpress, and to have such supplementary photographs added to the album as he might judge proper'. Unfortunately, no descriptive letterpress was provided, although further photographs were taken.

Recognition of the quality of the work was quickly apparent. In October 1877 the Town Council asked for a bound set of the photographs together with another set framed 'for hanging on the walls'. The Librarian of the Medical Faculty of the University also asked for a copy, his interest being the evidence the photographs provided 'on the medical and sanitary history of the city'. In December 1878, the year of the failure of the City of Glasgow Bank, the Trustees asked the Edinburgh publishers, Messrs. Nelson & Son, to bind the volumes of the photographs in Morocco and send copies to the Town Council and to the Trustees, as well as to some of the officials. Thus the Glasgow City Improvements Trust in effect published the first edition of 100 quarto size copies.

In 1864, Sir Joseph Wilson Swan invented a new method of printing, involving the use of finely produced carbon, which produced a print of near-permanent quality. Thomas Annan bought the Scottish rights of this process, and used it for the second edition of *Old Closes and Streets*, published in Glasgow apparently around 1877/8. J. A. Fisher has observed[7] that in this edition there was 'achieved rich sombre effects which, by their deep shadows, could suggest degrees of decay lacking in the comparative clarity of the previous edition'.

This fin-de-siècle effect, however, was 'accentuated by the regrettable addition of elaborate cloud effects', and some 'ghost' figures were taken out.

The photogravure process, called heliogravure by its inventor Carl Klic of Vienna, allowed the printed carbon-tissue of the Swan process to be transferred to copper plates. Annan went to Vienna and obtained the rights from Klic, and in 1883 also obtained the Scottish rights of the photogravure process two years before any English photographer followed his example. The photogravure process was used in the third edition of 1900, which carried notes by Annan's fellow photographer, William Young. I have used the second edition for the prints in this anthology, since, despite the picturesque clouds, the detail is much sharper.

This anthology also contains examples of work from some of Annan's other publications. His *The Old Country Houses of the Old Glasgow Gentry*, which had a text by three once-eminent but now forgotten Glaswegians, was published by Maclehose, the University publisher, in 1870 in an edition of 100 copies. A second edition followed in 1878, this time of 225 copies. In the introduction to the second edition, the three authors collectively said: 'Glasgow has seen great changes since this book was published eight years ago. A man who had lived here all his life until then might today be set down in many parts of the City without having an idea where he was.' Though Glasgow had changed considerably as a result of Georgian development, until the clearance of the mediaeval city there had been no previous wholesale inner city replacement. Some of those who did not have to live in the slums felt that it 'severed many a link with the past'. The evident popularity of Annan's photographs was therefore, in Mosley's words, 'a part of the conservative spirit of a depressed period'[8] following which it was feared there might again be 'a great tidal wave' of further change.

Annan's *Memorial of the Old College of Glasgow*, published by Maclehose in 1871, contains not only studies of the College itself but portraits of the professors. I have included Annan's study of Professor Gairdner, because of his Public Health connection and of Professor Harry Rainy, the Professor of Medical Jurisprudence, as an arresting study of a Scottish Victorian intellectual. From Annan's *Photographs of Glasgow*, a volume of 30 views of the city published in 1868 with descriptive letterpress by the Reverend A. G. Forbes, I have selected his photograph of the West End Park, a recreational facility laid out from designs by Sir Joseph Paxton on land purchased by the Corporation from the Woodlands and Kelvingrove Estates in the 1850s.

The images Thomas Annan presented to the Trustees of the City Improvements and to the city fathers were not simply the dry record which doubtless they had expected to receive, but a series of individual works of art in photography, revealing a compositional skill and ability to catch atmosphere only matched in Scotland at that time by, in addition to some of those already named, Alexander Johnston, who was operating among the fishing community of the north of Scotland from his studio at Wick, in Caithness.

In spite of the early appearance of a few photographers like Annan and the other known early Scottish practitioners, photography, by its very nature, has tended to wrap itself in anonymity. Surviving Victorian and Edwardian photographs are, for the most part, either commercial postcards, 'one-off' publications like *Govan: Past and Present* by the local draper/photographer John Irvin, commemorating the visit to Glasgow by H.R.H. the Prince of Wales in 1907, or random memories 'snapped' by family amateurs. It is therefore all too rarely possible to give credit with certainty to the photographic artists whose cameras, intentionally or not, have preserved for us otherwise uncapturable moments in time from the days of yesteryear. Literature, music and painting preserve for us in infinite depth the 'feel' of their particular era; what is ultimately of timeless significance about it. What photography excels in capturing, though, are single instants in the long succession of continuously fleeting experiences which together add up to the usually unremarkable lifetime of the average man and woman. Fortunately, these were precisely the qualities which inspired two Glasgow photographers of later Victorian times, one an enthusiastic lifelong amateur, the other an engine driver turned professional photographer of necessity in later life.

The amateur was William Young, RSW (1845–1916). He was born at Catrine in Ayrshire, the son of the agent of the Western Bank at Catrine and the grandson of the local foundry master. When the Western Bank collapsed, partly as a result of its attempt to defeat the Edinburgh banks by offering over-the-odds interest rates and making less than prudent loans, Young senior transferred to the Exchange Square branch of the Royal Bank, now the Glasgow Head Office. The son was educated in Glasgow. There may have been family money behind him, but throughout his life he seems to have earned his living as a much-praised popular artist, principally in watercolours. In 1884, *The Bailie* commented that:

> while his landscapes have distinguished an uncompromising truth as to local form and colour, he succeeds, at the same time, in giving them a tinge of poetry, in colouring them with some of the sentiment which pervades his own nature.

As a young man he had attended classes in drawing and had studied painting at the Glasgow School of Art. He was often to be seen with his easel in the countryside outside the City, particularly near the Dunbartonshire village of Old Kilpatrick. Here his friend William Dennistoun lived, and at Dennistoun's home, in 1867, the two friends launched the Glasgow Art Club, Young becoming its first secretary.

A man of wide interests, Young was also an enthusiastic string player in the Glasgow Amateur Orchestral Society, a keen participator in chamber music and a lively observer of the life around him, compiling some 40 scrap books, many of which contained prints of his own photographs along with cuttings about local events and personalities clipped from magazines and newspapers. The scrap books are now in the Glasgow Room of The Mitchell Library. Young seems to have been particularly active as a photographer during the 1870s. As late as 1900, he provided his introduction to the third edition of Annan's *The Old Closes and Streets of Glasgow*.

By comparison, William Graham (1845–1914) would seem to have led a much less privileged existence. He was born in what is now the Springburn district of Glasgow and lived there all his days, working for the North British Railway Company. In 1893, while an engine driver, he supported a strike, as a result of which he left the Company's employment; whether voluntarily or otherwise is not recorded. For his last 11 years he earned his living as a photographer, turning his hobby into his profession.

He, too, had wide interests. He was a founder member of the Old Glasgow Club, and brought into the focus of his camera everything from carthorses to cathedrals, from churches to rich mansions, street scenes and shops; above all, though, people, apparently recording the despair of destitution with the same objectivity as the pomp of civic dignity. He also photographed works of art, etchings, and pieces of sculpture and sometimes even made his own rephotographed copies of the images of others, thus making it difficult to label a particular image as certainly a Graham original.

Two years after Graham's death, the convener of the Libraries Committee of Glasgow Corporation, Baillie T. H. Hutchison, bought the Graham collection privately and presented it to The Mitchell Library to commemorate his years of convenership. A little later, Graham's widow handed over some contemporary prints, made from the negatives by then in the Library's possession. Besides the prints, the Graham collection consisted of 3000 glass negatives covering portraits of over 300 Glasgow characters and many views of Glasgow streets and buildings.

While it is sometimes difficult precisely to date photographs that have survived through chance preservation in a family trunk or loft, the earliest photograph in this book – from the Graham collection – was probably taken about 1850. The latest – inevitably, indeed the majority – come from the closing years of King Edward's reign. Thus the anthology spans the 20 years or so when Glasgow rose to its peak of assured prosperity, before beginning in the 1870s a decline so gradual that it was scarcely even noticeable by the time the 1914–18 War broke out.

During its long years of expansion and overall growth – from the eighteenth century almost to the end of the nineteenth – the fabric of Glasgow usually established a certain homogeneity of architectural style, at least from district to district. Almost everything was newly designed. Victorians may not have produced a new architectural style of their own, but they were wonderfully inventive in reinterpreting and creating variations upon the great styles of antiquity, shamelessly combining them where it suited their purpose. Local architects who made use of native materials were normally employed, and the standard of craftsmanship was normally high. The result could be, at its best, a pleasing homogeneity of excellence. That consistency began to be eroded after the First World War. It simply collapsed under the social, economic and environmental pressures which all but engulfed the city in the wake of the 1939–45 War.

Glasgow has always been much less frequently photographed than its more tourist-conscious 'rival', Edinburgh; perhaps because Glaswegians have only comparatively recently awakened to the tourist potential of their own city, possessing what Sir John Betjamin described as 'the finest Victorian architectural heritage in Europe'. Glasgow, however, has attracted a sufficient number of levelled lenses, especially with social subject matter in focus, for a fair heritage of images to have come down to us. Not surprisingly, they cover the extremes of affluence and poverty.

For the majority of its population, neither Victorian nor Edwardian Glasgow can have been a pleasant place to live in. Victorian values allowed little patience for weakness or the fruits of miscalculation. The assured front of success was what mattered. We should therefore not allow nostalgia to cloud unrealistically our enjoyment of these Victorian and Edwardian images. Both pre-war twentieth-century Georgian and post-second-war modern Elizabethan Glasgow have suffered economic decline and experienced a good deal of unnecessary havoc wrought upon the fabric of the City. The fine buildings destroyed are, of course, quite irreplaceable: but lessons have been learned. The conservation of the best of the City's Victorian and Edwardian man-made heritage has become almost a popular cause, even if the major stimulus to such a reappraisal may have been an intense dislike of much of what has been put up during the past 40 years. In spite of anti-social and impractical high-rise tower blocks and boring bargain-basement kit-assembled office blocks, for most Glaswegians their City is now a better place to live in than the architecturally more unified and imposing Glasgow that existed a hundred years ago.

Notes

1 The Carron Iron Works, some three miles south of Falkirk, had been founded by Dr Roebuck of Sheffield in 1760. Without having made any prior arrangement, Burns turned up to visit them on Sunday 26th April 1787. On being refused admission, he scratched some harsh lines on the window of a Falkirk inn.

2 The employment of planners only became mandatory for Scottish local authorities in 1946. Many of the early planners were hastily seconded from other disciplines and hurriedly trained.

3 John Hannary: *A Moment in Time: Scottish Contributions to Photography 1840–1920*, Glasgow, 1983. For the pre-history of photography and its evolution from the camera obscura, see Helmut Gernsheim: *The Origins of Photography*, London, 1982. See also Beaumont Newall: *The History of Photography*, London, 1972, and Ian Jeffrey: *Photography – A Concise History*, London, 1981.

4 For fuller details see Robert Taylor: *George Washington Wilson*, London, 1981.

5 Introduction to *Thomas Annan: Photographs of the Old Closes and Streets of Glasgow, 1868–1877*, New York, 1977.

6 J.A. Fisher: *A Guide to the Published Photography of Thomas Annan*, The Mitchell Library, 1977.

7 ibid.

8 ibid.

1. A number of early photographs of Glasgow street scenes by Thomas Annan, all taken around 1866, have survived. This fine view of the Trongate looks east from the Tron Steeple. The Tolbooth Steeple is on the left, beyond the piazza of the Tontine Hotel. The statue outside the hotel is of King William III, presented to the City in 1735 by James Macrae, a former Governor of Madras. It now stands in Cathedral Square.

2. The Saltmarket from the Bridgegate, as seen by Thomas Annan. Early photography was not very good at catching moving people (because of long exposures), or focussing large groups in depth. Note the Vintner's sign outside the shop on the left.

top left **3.** Hope Street, looking north. This photograph from the Graham collection, perhaps taken three decades later than **1** and **2**, shows the tower of the Central Station and Hotel. Two cabs seem to be making their way towards the Station.

bottom left **4.** At the heart of the City of Glasgow, then as now, is Glasgow Cathedral, here photographed by Annan. From mediaeval times, the Cathedral was at the heart of Glasgow life. It is still used for the official 'kirkings' of newly elected local authorities. To the left is Robert Adam's Royal Infirmary, built on the site of the Bishop's Castle, but replaced in 1897.

5. The University, or Old College, founded in 1450 and opened the following year, met at first in the crypt of the Cathedral until James, the first Lord Hamilton, provided ground for the erection of buildings. The area was augmented by later gifts, including church land donated by Mary, Queen of Scots. Jacobean buildings went up between 1630 and 1660, and survived until the opening of the new University on Gilmorehill in 1870. This view of the handsome High Street façade, with a cab opposite the main entrance, was first published in *Roman Memorials of the Old College* in 1871.

6. The entrance to the Old College. Its destruction, from the hygienic standpoint of more than a century later, still seems the most grievous architectural loss Glasgow has yet suffered.

right **7.** Another Annan study: the entrance into the Outer Court. The entablature contains the Arms of Glasgow, incorporating the bell and salmon, with the addition of the University's book.

8. The architect of the University on Gilmorehill was Sir George Gilbert Scott (1810–1877). Various designs were submitted, including a noble one by Alexander Thomson. Scott's was described at the time as 'a magnificent design in the domestic early English style with Scottish or Flemish features of a later date', the foundation stone being laid by the Prince of Wales on 8 October 1868. The Bute Hall was the gift in 1877 of the Marquess of Bute; the Randolph Hall, 1878–84, was also a gift, from the shipbuilder Charles Randolph. Yet another shipbuilder, Sir William Pearce, paid for the removal of the main entrance and part of the front of the Old College and its re-erection at what was then the main approach to the new University. Again, we are indebted to Thomas Annan for recording the historic moment when the Professors formally processed out of the Old College for the last time.

top **9.** In 1864, the lands of Gilmorehill and Donaldshill were bought for £98,400 along with the lands of Clayslaps. Part of these estates became Kelvingrove Park. The other part was used for the building of the Western Infirmary. The old house of Gilmorehill, built by Robert Bogle in 1802, was not lived in after 1822, having been sold by Bogle's son, Archibald, to the Glasgow Western Cemetery Company. The Estate was never used as a burial ground, however, but was resold at a profit to the College of Glasgow, who began work on the University in 1866. Shortly before its demolition, Thomas Annan photographed Gilmorehill House, with construction work on the University proceeding in the background.

below **10.** There was an uneasy feeling in Victorian times that a God-fearing seat of learning must have a spire. The later fretted spire, so designed not to overload the tower, was added in 1886, the gift of two Glaswegians, Andrew Cunninghame, the Deputy Town Clerk, and James Marshall.

11. The Tontine Hotel consisted of an hotel, a coffee room for subscribers and an assembly hall. It was built in two stages, the eastern half being finished by 1736 and the western half in 1760. Both were bought by the Tontine Society in 1787 and converted into the Hotel photographed here. The Hotel was the haunt of the Tobacco Lords, the coffee room a recognized place of business. The Grand Ball with which the reconstructed hotel of 1781 was opened was the first of many such assemblies held there, although in 1796 the Tontine's social supremacy for such functions was challenged by Robert Adam's New Assembly Rooms in Ingram Street extension, the site on which the General Post Office now stands. The decline of the central area of the City due to overcrowding and the Highland and Irish influx led to the abandonment of the Tontine as an hotel in the 1850s. It was turned into shops and offices, but totally gutted by fire in 1912.

12. There were, of course, less elegant hostelries. The rear of one of them, the Green Dyke Tavern, in Green Street, by 1898 suggests a picturesque decrepitude, though it can hardly have been pleasant to drink in.

13. The Celtic influx produced the intolerable slums of the 1840s, '50s and early '60s. The City Improvement Act of 1866, twice amended (in 1873 and 1880), operated for 15 years and empowered the Town Council 'to alter, widen, divert, or altogether efface the number of old streets and construct new ones'. Twelve old streets disappeared and nine new ones were formed. Thomas Annan's studies of 1868 preserved the squalor to which the old closes of the mediaeval sites had sunk. This is Close Number 29, Saltmarket.

14. Close Number 37, High Street.

15. The move westwards, which began in the 1840s with the construction of what is now the Park Conservation Area, extended beyond the Kelvin with the development of Kelvinside. This photograph of 1870 shows the first and second bridges over the Kelvin, both disappearing when the present bridge was erected in 1891. The graceful spire of Landsdowne Church, the slimmest of the City's many spires, is the work of the architect John Honeyman (1831–1914) and went up in 1862. The Great Western Road, tree-lined and with the amenity of the Royal Botanic Gardens, laid out in 1842, was the scene of a satirical sketch in the 1890s, published in *The Bailie*, a popular Glasgow magazine, showing an elegant parade of Sunday fashion.

The ladies are in the wasp-waisted bustle skirts of the time and, like the top-hatted gentlemen, would have mostly come from the handsome terraces such as these two, standing back from the main thoroughfare.

16. On the left of this photograph, from Fleming's *Kelvinside* (1894) is Charles Wilson's Kirklee Terrace, first called High Windsor Terrace when completed in 1845. On the right is Belhaven Terrace West by James Thomson (1845–1905), put up between 1866 and 1869 and now almost entirely a University Hall of Residence. Note the carriage steps to assist passengers entering or alighting from cabs. Many of these carriage steps survived into the years of my boyhood, when the motor cars of the 1920s and '30s frequently damaged their low-slung running-boards against them.

SMOKING
SMOKING

top left **17.** Of all the terraces along Great Western Road none quite equalled the stately palace-like block of Alexander 'Greek' Thomson's Great Western Terrace (1869). Thomson was as much influenced by Old Testament motifs as by those of antiquity, but in fact never travelled further afield than the Island of Arran. The houses in Great Western Terrace were probably only exceeded in spacious grandeur by those in Charles Wilson's Park Circus. One of the original owners in Great Western Terrace was the shipowner Sir William Burrell, whose magnificent arts bequest to Glasgow forms the Burrell Collection.

bottom left **18.** One of the features of the Botanic Gardens is the domed Kibble Palace, an iron-framed glass structure which once stood in the grounds of the Coulport house of a wealthy industrialist, John Kibble. In 1872 he sold it to Glasgow. It was extended for its opening the following year. At first it was used as a concert and lecture hall, although the humidity of the interior makes this use somewhat impracticable, but it still houses a fine collection of neo-classical sculpture by Victorian Masters and, of course, varied plant life.

above **19.** Kelvinside House, built in 1760 for the Dunmore family. It disappeared a century later as the district of Kelvinside developed over the Estate.

20. The Victorians built themselves many fine churches. One of them in the West End, Hillhead Parish Church (1875/6), now Belmont-Hillhead, echoed the French Sainte-Chapelle theme, unusual in a Presbyterian church. It is the work of James Sellars (1843–1888). It was still fairly new when this anonymous photograph was taken.

21. Kelvingrove House, on the banks of the Kelvin, was built in 1782 by Patrick Colquhoun from plans by Robert Adam. It was demolished in 1900 to make way for the 1901 Glasgow Exhibition buildings.

22. Nearer the City, in the 1840s and '50s, on the hill between Woodlands and the West End Park, later Kelvingrove Park, great quadrants and terraces were built, crowned by Charles Wilson's Park Circus. The West End Park, along the banks of the River Kelvin, was at first confined to the east side of the river and was constructed of land purchased by Glasgow Corporation in 1853. It was laid out by Sir Joseph Paxton. The park was extended after the purchase of the Clayslaps and Kelvingrove lands in 1881. This photograph of about 1880 shows Park Circus (1857/9), Park Terrace (1855) and the tower of the Free Church College (1856) by Charles Wilson, later Trinity College and now redeveloped to become office and private accommodation.

23. Back now to the City centre. On the right of this photograph, *c.* 1890, is the City Hall, built by George Murray (1806–1841) in 1840 for a limited liability company but subsequently re-roofed, added to and much improved in 1855 by John Carrick (1819–1890) and in 1907 by J. A. D. Houston. Used during World War II as the headquarters of food rationing in the City, the building was extensively restored by Archibald Jury, the City Architect, in 1968 some years after fire destroyed St Andrews Hall. The church at the top of the street, since 1953 the combined St Paul's (Outer High) and St David's (Ramshorn) was built in 1824 by the Birmingham architect Thomas Rickman (1776–1841), an early example in Scotland of the revival of Early Decorated Style. Note the schoolboy delivering his cans of milk.

24. Of the many churches of Secessionist persuasion in Glasgow, one of the most interesting was Bridgegate United Free Church, built in 1860. It was the last church to possess an outside pulpit. This gave opportunity for the Minister to attack those of other religious persuasions, principally the Catholics. Its use was banned by Magistrates because such sectarian preaching led to riot and obstruction in the streets. The church was demolished in 1915 to make way for road widening. The old Merchant House steeple, in the background, survives as part of the late twentieth-century Bridgegate Development. Mitchell's, whose thick black tobacco is advertised in the shop window, for many years manufactured in Glasgow their Prize Crop cigarettes from a factory latterly in Alexandra Parade.

25. Also in the Merchant City is the County Building and Court Houses, built as the result of a competition by the architects William Clarke and George Bell in 1844 as the Sheriff Court. There was an addition in 1871 and some later none-too-happy alterations. This photograph of the Wilson Street façade probably dates from the 1870s. Note the elegant gas street lamps.

26. One of the finest Victorian churches, photographed here by Thomas Annan in the 1870s, is Alexander Thomson's St Vincent Street Church, owned by the local authority, now under restoration, but leased to a Free Church. The commission to build this church was secured by Alexander's brother, George, who is said to have had a hand in the design of the tower, with its suggestion of Old Testament influence. The podium which carries the church contains halls and other buildings. A late twentieth-century building now occupies the site of the wooden stables, but the modern building was so designed as not to obscure the view of the church.

ERY STABLES

27. The City Chambers design was chosen after two competitions. The winning award went to a London Scot, William Young (1843–1900) who erected it between 1883 and 1889 at a total cost, including the site, of £520,000. The foundation stone was laid on 6 October 1883 by Lord Provost Ure and, as can be seen from this contemporary photograph, the securing of a good view of the proceedings took precedence over considerations of personal safety. The opening ceremony was in due course performed by Queen Victoria on 22 August 1886.

28. This German photograph, published by Stengell & Son in 1902, gives some idea of the magnificence of the building, with its four corner towers, central tower and pediment carrying a statue of Queen Victoria supported on each side by female figures representing England, Scotland, Ireland and Wales. On the apex of the pediment is the figure of Liberty supported by Riches and Honour, two personifications who have in reality not always got on well together. The Italianate interior is of rich splendour, the great marble staircase sweeping up to the second floor, which contains the halls and reception rooms.

29. The busy corporate life that kept the official, public side of things going bustled about the surrounding streets. Argyle Street, shown here in 1896, was then as now a popular shopping centre.

30. Another view of Argyle Street and the end of Buchanan Street. To the left of this photograph is the corner of St Enoch Subway Station, now the Travel Centre. The cable-hauled underground, originally built by a private company in 1896, was not entirely satisfactory, but it survived until 1935, when Glasgow Corporation took it over and electrified it. It was completely modernized in 1978/79. The Bonanza Drapery Store in due course became Arnott's. The ramp to the right led to the Glasgow and South Western Railway's St Enoch Station and Hotel.

ALL CARS
STOP HERE

INTERNATIONAL
EXHIBITION

top left **31.** One of Scotland's most popular shopping streets was Renfield Street, shown in a postcard, *c.* 1900, by E. T. W. Dennis of London. The famous store R. & W. Forsyth survived until the 1960s. An early motor delivery van with solid tyres is turning into Gordon Street.

centre left **32.** Of Glasgow's four Victorian railway stations, only Queen Street and Central Station survive. Buchanan Street and St Enoch were both demolished in post-Second World War years. Central Station, the main line terminal for the London Midland and Scottish railway to London and Birmingham was, and still is, the most important. It was opened by the Caledonian Company in 1879, extended in 1890, in 1906 and is now being extensively reconstructed internally. Adjacent to it in 1884 rose the Central Station Hotel by Sir Rowand Anderson (1834–1921). It was extended back along Hope Street by James Miller in 1907. The covered entrance to the Hotel can just be seen in this Valentine postcard of 1907. Opposite the entrance is the top of an early motor taxi.

bottom left **33.** This Collectercard view of the Trongate is dated *c.* 1905. The advertisement on the entrance to the railway station building advertising trains 'every few minutes' to the International Exhibition at Kelvingrove suggests that 1901 might be a more accurate date. The Tron Kirk Steeple with its clock is all that survives of the Tron Church, built in 1593–5 and completed in 1630–6, but steeple apart, burned down in 1793. The re-built church, now the Tron Theatre, was constructed a little apart from the steeple.

34. Throughout later Victorian years and the whole of the Edwardian era Charing Cross, which linked Sauchiehall Street with Woodlands Road, the road to Maryhill and Springburn and the road to Partick and the West, was a popular and important shopping centre. In this photograph, *c.* 1910, a prominent feature is the Grand Hotel. It was built between 1875 and 1878 by John Duncanson and opened by him as the most luxurious hotel in the City. In its heyday it was opulently fashionable. As a very small boy in the 1920s, the present writer danced Lancers and Quadrilles in its still elegant ballroom at the annual dancing class pupils' demonstrations of Miss Brown and later, of her successor, Miss Webster. Both ladies were descendants of the eighteenth-century Ballroom Directresses. The German composer Eugene D'Albert, still remembered, at least in Germany, for his opera *Tiefland*, was born in the building (1864), his mother, a travelling virtuoso pianist, having got her "dates" wrong. In the background is the curve of Charing Cross Mansions, built in the French style in 1911 by Sir J. J. Burnet (1857–1938).

In order to make way for the City motorway ring road, the Grand Hotel and the second tenement building on the right were demolished in 1968. Only the fountain on the left, erected in 1896 by public subscription to commemorate Sir Charles Cameron, M.P., survives. It is known affectionately as Glasgow's 'Leaning Tower', because of its tilted angle. The whole appearance of Charing Cross has been drastically altered; disfigured, some might say, not by the ring road itself, which is sunken, but by a hideous concrete bridge connecting nothing and leading nowhere, optimistically intended by the Planners of the day to be a kind of shop-lined version of the Venetian 'Bridge of Sighs'!

35. Woodlands Road and the Gothic Woodlands Church, by John Burnett Senior, in 1874, as it looked at the turn of the century, complete with its Burne-Jones windows, since removed. The Glasgow tenement was the standard form of flatted accommodation in the City from about 1840 until 1914. Woodlands Road connected Charing Cross with the University, and with Great Western Road.

36. Also connecting with Charing Cross through the western sector of Sauchiehall Street was Partick. Partick Bridge – the third on the site over the River Kelvin, a tributary of the Clyde that ran down the western edge of the early-nineteenth-century City – was erected in 1877, designed and built by R. B. Bell and D. Miller. Its predecessor of 1577 stood alongside it until 1895. The various styles of *c.* 1900 horse-drawn commercial vehicles is interesting. The building which forms the centrepiece of this postcard photograph is the Kelvingrove Art Galleries, built as part of the 1901 Exhibition. Although an almost absurd amalgam of architectural styles and decorative motifs, it houses one of the finest collections of pictures in the United Kingdom and is particularly rich in the work of the French impressionists and, of course, the group of painters known as the 'Glasgow School'.

37. Cabs and, to the rear, a horse-drawn bus move westwards over Kelvin Bridge and along the Great Western Road towards Kelvinside in 1896. Behind the spire of Landsdowne Church is that of St Mary's Episcopalian Cathedral. The Cathedral was built by Sir George Gilbert Scott between 1871 and 1874, but the spire was completed by his son, John Aldred Scott.

38. Bridges have formed a feature of Glasgow since mediaeval times. The iron girder bridge carries rail traffic into Central Station and was finished in 1878. The third Jamaica Bridge, seen under construction in 1899, is 20 feet wider than Telford's second bridge of 1833, which it replaced and which in turn had taken the place of a 1772 bridge. The photograph was taken by an executive of the railway company.

39. Stockwell Bridge, opened in 1854, when it was known as Victoria Bridge. It replaced the Old Glasgow Bridge, taken down in 1845. Again, an anonymous railway archive photograph dating from the late 1890s.

40. As the former villages which fringed the boundaries of Glasgow were gradually absorbed, they were redeveloped. This view is of Main Street, Govan, dating from 1872. The combination of thatched roofs and street lamps, albeit sparsely planted, is interesting.

41. An even earlier Govan photograph of the Waverley Tavern, in Water Row, dating from *c.* 1860. It appears to have attracted some prosperously dressed customers.

42. Before Glasgow moved westwards, an attempt was made to develop the South Side of the Clyde. Unfortunately, the arrival of industry, which in these days could establish itself wherever it chose, soon led to the sooty discomforts of mixed usage and to the decline in residential popularity of such developments as Carlton Place. By the 1880s the houses in Charlotte Street had lost their elegant ambience, but had not yet degenerated into the slum condition which overtook them and their like in nearby Gorbals, leading to their demolition soon after the end of the Second World War.

top left **43.** North of the City, Springburn had an industrial base in the locomotive and heavy engineering industries. The main street still looked fairly rural in 1898, when this photograph was taken. The castellated building on the hill is Breeze's Tower, named after a Victorian quarry-master owner but built by a sea captain for his retirement *c.* 1830 and conserved in our own day.

45. Near the mediaeval City centre, a few streets escaped the Glasgow Improvement Trust's attentions. This photograph, taken *c.* 1902, shows a thatched house with forestairs and a corner-shop dairy.

bottom left **44.** By the 1880s, the development of Pollokshields had given the South Side a new residential desirability. Few general photographs have survived of early Pollokshields, the spacious gardens making effective group photography difficult.

46. Another survivor, this time in the Gallowgate, *c.* 1903, its Dutch-style chimney gable presumably providing the landlord with advertising income. The Hippodrome was opened in 1902 and closed in 1904, and was located at 326 Sauchiehall Street. The zoo was opened in 1897, but by 1903 stood in New City Road. The Hippodrome in Sauchiehall Street became Hengler's Circus in 1904.

47. By the turn of the century, the tenement was the favourite form of housing for those who could not afford individual mansions or terraced dwellings. At first, tenements were built of local grey sandstone, but by the beginning of the twentieth century local quarries had become exhausted and red sandstone was shipped in from Dumfriesshire or the Island of Arran. This nineteenth-century photograph of Dowanhill Park and School has early red sandstone tenements in the rearground and older grey sandstone terraced houses to the left.

48. Seventeenth-, eighteenth- and nineteenth-century houses sharing the south side of the Drygate in 1906.

49. Tenements in Airlie Gardens, Partickhill, in 1908. Some tenements had occasional main door flats, but the entrance to most of the flats was through a shared tiled close entrance. Such a close can be seen to the left of the picture.

50. A few of Glasgow's great houses, over whose estates the City expanded, survived for a time at least. Garscadden House, built in 1723 and pictured here by Thomas Annan, one of the most impressive, was owned by the Colquhouns of Killermont. In 1950 it was converted into service flats. The story is told of a convivial group of eighteenth-century Lairds – by custom called by the name of their estates – met together for an evening's drinking. 'What gars Garscadden luick sae gash?' (makes Garscadden look so pale), one asked of his neighbour. 'Aw aye,' came the answer. 'He's been wi' his Maker thae twa hoors or mair, but I didna like tae disturb guid company.'

51. Whitehill, also photographed by Annan, was the home of the Tobacco Lord John Glassford, after whom a central City street is named. It was demolished in the 1860s to make way for a well-known school of the same name, now also demolished.

52. A few houses of the old Glasgow gentry still survive. Tollcross, again photographed by Annan, still surrounded by the park of the same name, was acquired by Glasgow Corporation in 1896. Built in 1848, Tollcross was the home of the Dunlop family. In post-Second World War years it housed the delightful Museum of Childhood, but this fell victim to environmental restrictions on local authorities in the late 1970s and '80s. The future of the house is still uncertain.

53. In many ways the greatest of all Glasgow houses was, and is, Pollok House, designed by William Adam in 1847–52, on the right bank of the White Cart river, for the Maxwell family, later Stirling Maxwell. It stands on an estate given by David I to Walter, the High Steward, coming to Maxwells in the thirteenth century. The entrance hall, wings, terraces and garden pavilions of Pollok were added by Sir Rowand Anderson from 1892 onwards. The house and grounds were given by the Stirling Maxwell family to Glasgow Corporation in 1967, though the grounds had been open to the public since 1911. They are now administered in conjunction with the National Trust for Scotland. Within them has been erected Barry Gasson's fine Burrell Collection Gallery. The house itself, now administered by Juliet Kinchin for Glasgow Art Galleries, contains the remarkable Stirling Maxwell collection of pictures, including two El Grecos and several Blakes. Much visited, it remains a remarkable rural retreat to survive in the midst of the surrounding City.

54. One unusually fortunate old Glasgow dwelling is Haggs Castle, built for Sir John Maxwell of Pollok in 1585. It fell into disuse and ruin when it was replaced by Pollok House. Here, a party of gentlemen is seen visiting Haggs Castle during the summer of 1860. The woman in the cottage must either have had a large family, or perhaps have 'taken in' gentlemen's washing.

55. Haggs Castle was restored in the late nineteenth century. It was used as a house in 1910, the date of the photograph, subsequently turned into flats, and is now a History Museum designed for children rather than a museum of childhood.

top right **56.** A striking image of a young mother and her baby in a slum room, *c.* 1890.

bottom right **57.** An even more horrifying image of an old woman lying on the floor, taken in 1888.

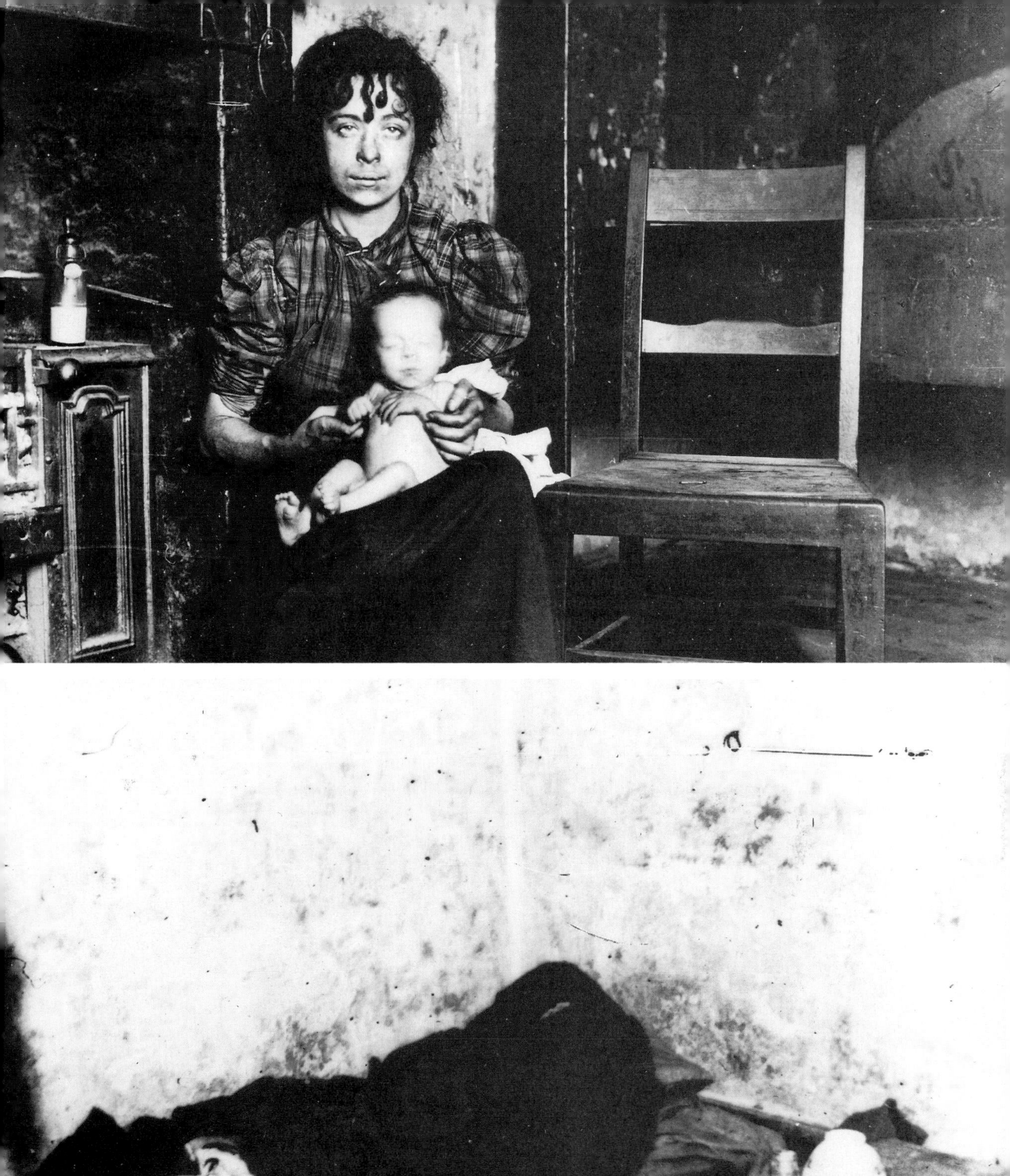

58. By contrast, these 1890s Gorbals children on the Main Street swings look robust and happy.

59. So, too, does this sturdy milkmaid, photographed on Blochairn Farm, Glenboig, around 1900.

60. Granny Wilson, *c.* 1900, the oldest member of Sighthill United Presbyterian Church. The kitchen range and the gas jet above it were typical of the period.

61. A contrasting *Art Nouveau* interior of about the same period, the study of the Reverend James Dickie of Springburn.

62. The cab (or cabriolet, to give it its full name) first appeared on Glasgow streets in the 1820s. One of the earliest Glasgow cab drivers, or 'cabbies', as they were called, was reputed to be George Haggarth, who died in 1905 at an advanced age.

right **63.** Before the general adoption of the water closet, ordure had to be emptied by dustmen. This work was usually undertaken at night. This photograph, taken around 1910, shows a dustman at work.

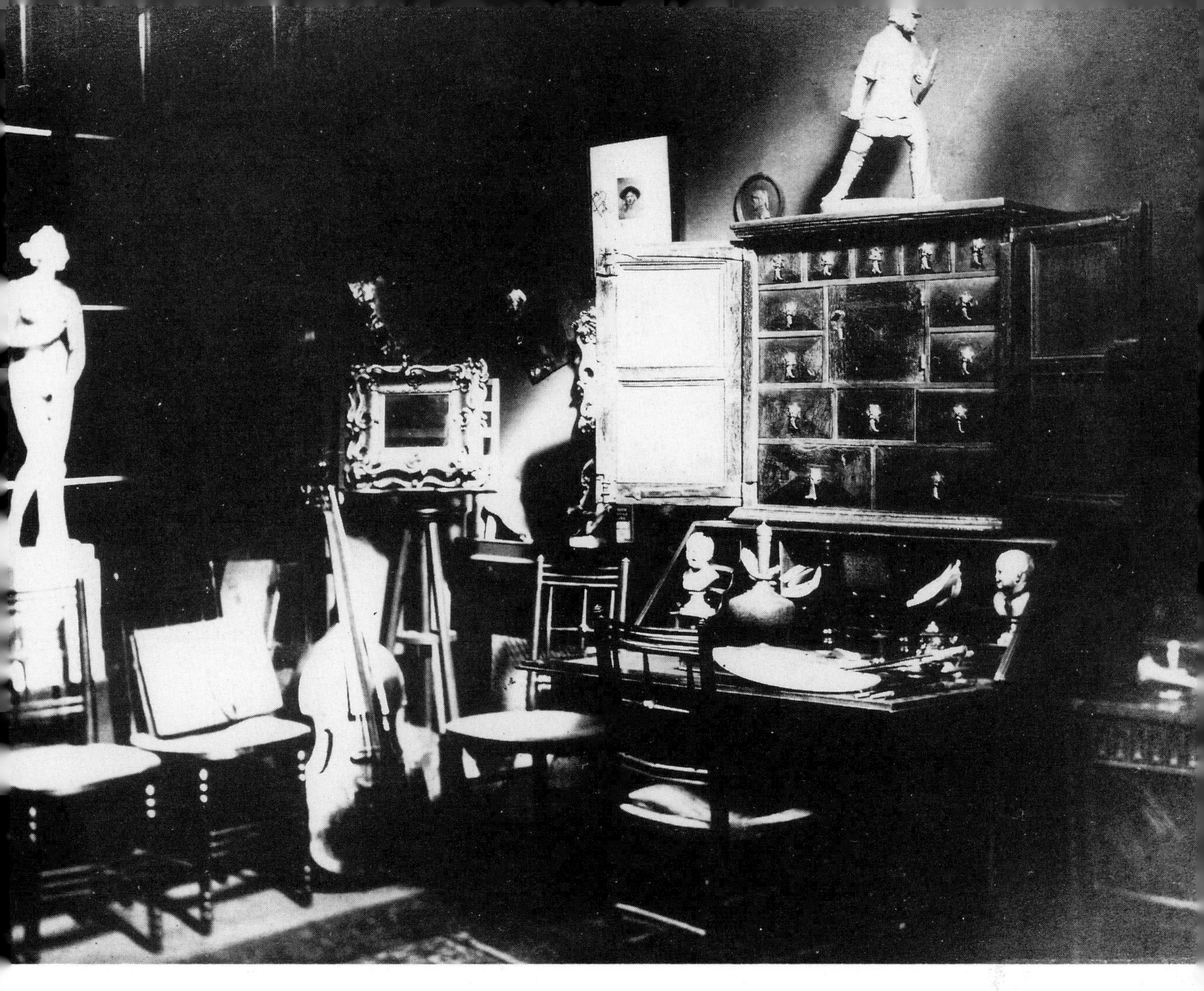

left **64.** The photographer William Young had his own portrait taken by his friend Hamish Hendry, probably in the 1880s.

65. A corner of William Young's studio at 65 West Regent Street, taken in 1886. It displays the variety of his artistic interests.

66. Thomas Annan took many distinguished portraits. One was of Sir William Gairdner, Professor of Practice of Medicine at Glasgow University from 1862 to 1900, and in 1864 appointed the City's first Public Health Officer.

67. Young Thomas Annan himself, taken on Christmas Eve 1857.

68. Another Annan study of almost Rembrandt-like intensity: Harry Rainy M.D., Professor of Forensic Medicine at Glasgow University from 1841 to 1872.

69. J. B. Fleming, who inherited the Kelvinside Estate from his father. An Edwardian dandy, he was an extrovert renowned for his swagger. He used this portrait as a frontispiece to his book *Kelvinside* (1894).

70. Expectations ran less high in Victorian times. Pleasures, for most, were simpler than now. Much use was made of parks and open spaces, like Cathedral Square. The small drinking fountain to the right came from the iron foundry of Walter Macfarlane, originally near the Saracen's Head in the Gallowgate, though latterly at Possil. Macfarlane's specialized in ornamental and cast iron work. Their range included bandstands, balconies, intricate gates, railings, seats, fountains and lamps. The tower in the background is that of Barony Free Church (1866), but became so delapidated by 1972 that it had to be demolished. The house behind the fountain to the left is Provand's Lordship, Glasgow's oldest house, a plain crow-stepped building dating from 1471 with wings added behind in 1670. Originally the clergy house of St Nicholas Hospital, it became the manse of the Prebend (or Provand) of Barlanark, was sold in 1906, and is now in local authority care and the museum.

71. Listening to the band was a popular pastime. Springburn Park possessed one of Macfarlane's ornamental bandstands.

top right **72.** Another favourite occupation was perambulating along Great Western Road, or walking in the Botanic Gardens, the main entrance to which is seen in this Annan photograph of 1905. The building with the two onion domes was the Botanic Gardens station of the railway line from Glasgow Central to Maryhill, closed in 1974. The station was unfortunately burned down in 1970.

bottom right **73.** For some families, pony riding was a popular pastime, as it was for this Springburn family photographed by Graham in 1899.

74. 1901 was an Exhibition year. In the foreground is one of the buildings erected especially for the 'Groveries', as the Exhibition was nicknamed. Behind it is the newly completed Art Galleries, which took more than 12 years to build and remained after the temporary buildings had been dismantled.

75. Though strictly speaking the 1911 Exhibition lies just outside our period, it was planned and mostly built in the final year of King Edward's reign. This Annan study shows a street scene, including the Mercat Cross, in the Exhibition's 'Scottish Tounie'.

76. Yachting was a favourite pastime among rich Glaswegians. Few informal photographs taken aboard the great yachts of Victorian and Edwardian times appear to have survived, but this one, probably taken in the 1880s, shows the yacht *Bloodhound* in full sail on the Clyde.

77. In winter time there were concerts and theatres to attend. The old Theatre Royal in Dunlop Street had stood for 80 years when it was destroyed by fire in 1862, following the last night of the pantomime for that season. It is said to have been better loved by Glasgow theatregoers than any other theatre before or since. It could not be re-built as its site was required for one of the railway bridges on which St Enoch Station was erected.

78. Apart from being smelly – untreated sewage was discharged into the Clyde from many Lanarkshire communities besides the City, Glasgow's first sewage farm not being installed until 1894 – the Clyde had a mud problem. The river, first artificially deepened from the estuary at Port Glasgow upriver to the Broomielaw in the 1770s by John Golborne, silted up so that its bed had to be regularly dredged. Then as now the mud thus recovered was then deposited by hoppers in deep water areas of the Firth. This early and badly stained photograph shows Dredger Number 1 at work; according to the Clyde Navigation's date, in 1875.

79. The St Enoch Hotel, built in a kind of neo-Gothic style by Thomas Wilson of Hampstead and Miles S. Gibson in 1880, was one of the City's most popular Victorian establishments. In this Annan photograph of 1900 it was still in its heyday. Sadly, it was demolished in 1977, leaving the toy-like Jacobean former subway station of the 1870s somewhat isolated, though ambitious plans for the cleared hotel-and-railway-station site exist.

80. The development of transport made it possible for working people to live further away from the factories that employed them and, for the better-off, facilities for shopping and pleasure-taking. Horse-drawn buses first appeared on Glasgow's streets in 1834. They ran between the river and canal harbours; the Broomielaw and Port Dundas and Port Eglinton. They were painted tartan, exposed on top, their straw-covered interior floors being steamy and no doubt rather smelly. This bus of the 1860s is seen at its Kelvingrove Street terminus.

81. Steamers were to improve in comfort and speed. In this photograph of 1896, the steamer on the left is the *Daniel Adamson*. The steamer which has pulled out in front of her is the Macbrayne Royal Mail steamer *Iona 3*, bound for Ardrishaig, along the Royal Route, a journey she performed with her sister ship the *Columba* throughout the late Victorian and Edwardian decades, and indeed into the Georgian era of the present writer's boyhood. The steamer at the quay is the *Benmore*. Beyond it are the Laird Line's Irish steamers. In mid-stream is one of the waterbuses known as cluthas.

82. Cluthas, so called after the Gaelic name for the Clyde, were introduced in 1884. Twelve in number, they ran from Stockwell Street bridge to eleven landing stages en route for Whiteinch, $3\frac{1}{2}$ miles away. The journey along the odoriferous river took 45 minutes and the fare was one old penny. In 1891, the cluthas' peak year, they carried $3\frac{1}{2}$ million passengers. The photograph shows Clutha Number 4. The cluthas were withdrawn in 1903.

83. One of the most popular pleasures open to Glaswegians was a trip 'doon the watter', as the Clyde was affectionately known, from Glasgow's Broomielaw to Dunoon or Rothesay. One of the earliest surviving photographs is this view of the 'Steamboat Wharf and River Clyde' from the corner of Jamaica Street, taken in 1852 by the industrialist John Kibble whose Kibble Palace is now in the Botanic Gardens. Kibble is believed to have used exceptionally large glass plates, all of which, however, have unfortunately disappeared. It is interesting to note that the proportion of paddle steamers and sailing ships is about equal.

84. While it is unduly fanciful to suppose that pre-television families passed their leisure hours in intellectual conversation or listening to great music, people were more adept at amusing themselves. Musical evenings were more common then than now, particularly among the wealthier classes. In this study by William Young, those participating in a musical evening at Gryffe Castle, Bridge of Weir – one of a number of villages outside Glasgow where Victorian industrialists made their homes – have been identified as, from left to right, Mr and Mrs Craig, Miss Roger (standing), Mrs Brown (at the piano) Mr Brown and Miss Broadfoot.

85. Springburn Choir in 1896, a Graham study. Choral singing was a popular Scots pastime, the repertoire often including Hamish MacCunn's settings of *The Lay of the Last Minstrel* and *Bonny Kilmenny*, the poems by Scott and Hogg respectively, as well as the common diet of sentimental ballads and part-songs and religious offerings like Stainer's *The Crucifixion*.

86. A Thomas Annan study of the Central Railway Station just after 1900 on Fair Saturday, traditionally the third Saturday of July. The bowlers outnumber the boaters, many of which appear to be worn by the ladies. The advertisements for Van Houten's Cocoa and Sunlight Soap may still be recalled by the older generation. The steamer in the poster is probably the first *Glen Sannox*, plying on the Arran run.

87. Advertising was perhaps less sophisticated than it is today, but no doubt Wilson's Advertising van, making known what was on offer at the Princess Theatre, Gorbals, now the Citizens' Theatre, was effective enough.

88. One of the early bus operators, Andrew Menzies (1822–1873) realized that vehicles running on street rails would move more smoothly than over the cobbled setts. Against a great deal of opposition, Menzies persuaded Glasgow Corporation to lay tramlines from St George's Cross to Eglinton Toll in 1869–70. His trams, painted in the clan colours, first ran on behalf of the Glagow Tramway Omnibus Company from St George's Cross to Eglinton Toll on 19 August 1872. In 1894 the Corporation decided not to renew the lease to his successor, John Duncan, but to run the services themselves. This photograph shows the first of the Corporation's trams.

89. Four years later the first electric tram ran on the Springburn route. Graham photographed it. The whole service was electrified by the opening of the 1901 Exhibition, when 332 trams were running.

BAKERS
ARMS.
HOT PIES
W. COVENTRY, WINE & SPIRIT MERCHANT.
STORE
ANDERSTON

W. D. NEWTON
FAMILY BUTCHER
J. GEMMELL 12
PALE ALE
SUNLIGHT SOAP

top left **90.** Two early horse-drawn buses.

bottom left **91.** The terminus at Springburn in the horse-drawn tram days of the early 1890s.

92. A Phase 2-type tram early in the century. The open upper deck front and rear portions of these vehicles was later covered in so that the whole of the top deck afforded shelter. Thus altered, many of these trams ran until the middle 1930s. Latterly, the fleet was augmented by the more luxurious Coronation-type vehicles. The trams were withdrawn in 1962.

top left **93.** After the Glasgow and Garnkirk coal-carrying line of 1831, which also conveyed passengers, the railways penetrated Glasgow in 1842, the first link being between the City and Edinburgh. The West Coast Glasgow to London line opened in 1848. Buchanan Street station, now demolished, opened in 1849 to serve the Highlands and was the Caledonian Railway's original terminal. Many of the engines were built in Glasgow. In this photograph from the Graham Collection a group of guards is grouped round a Caledonian Railway engine in Buchanan Street Station the year after it opened.

bottom left **94.** The Manager and Fireman at the Hyde Park Locomotive Works in 1862.

95. In spite of steam and electricity, the horse was used for commercial locomotion well into the 1930s, especially for drawing coal carts. This one dates from the 1890s and belonged to Cowlairs Co-operative Society.

96. This horse-drawn laundry cart was photographed around 1900.

97. Fires in the Springburn district were put out by a horse-drawn brigade. Here are the alert-looking firemen of 1895.

98. Rolling out the barrel, 1910-style, from Tennent's Brewery . . .

99. . . . and making sure the business stayed profitable: the Tennent accounting department, *c.* 1910.

top left **100.** Shipbuilding was a Clyde industry from the construction of the earliest of the wooden vessels to the days of the great Cunarders *Queen Mary* and *Queen Elizabeth*. Though unfortunately no longer so, the term *Clyde-built* was for long synonymous with unsurpassable craftmanship and unrivalled quality. This photograph shows an unidentified ship under construction at Govan, *c.* 1890.

bottom left **101.** Ships were coal-fired in these days and coaling them was a major operation. This picture of a coaling siding at Glasgow's Rothesay Docks dates from *c.* 1900.

102. While most of Glasgow's coal came from Lanarkshire, coal was mined in the West End of Glasgow in mediaeval times. This Newcomen Steam Winding Engine operated at Frame Colliery, Rutherglen, then on the outskirts of the City but now within its boundaries.

103. The servicing of old locomotives and the building of new ones was a major industry in the Cowlairs and Springburn districts. This Victorian study shows blacksmith John Kerr and hammerman A. Marshall in the Cowlairs Locomotive Works.

104. A view of the Hydepark Locomotive Works in 1862. It was to expand greatly before the century's end, making engines for the railways of the world.

105. John Robertson, the designer, with the engine of the first practical paddle steamer to sail on the Clyde, the *Comet*, which crossed the estuary for the first time in 1812 with its designer, Henry Bell, aboard.

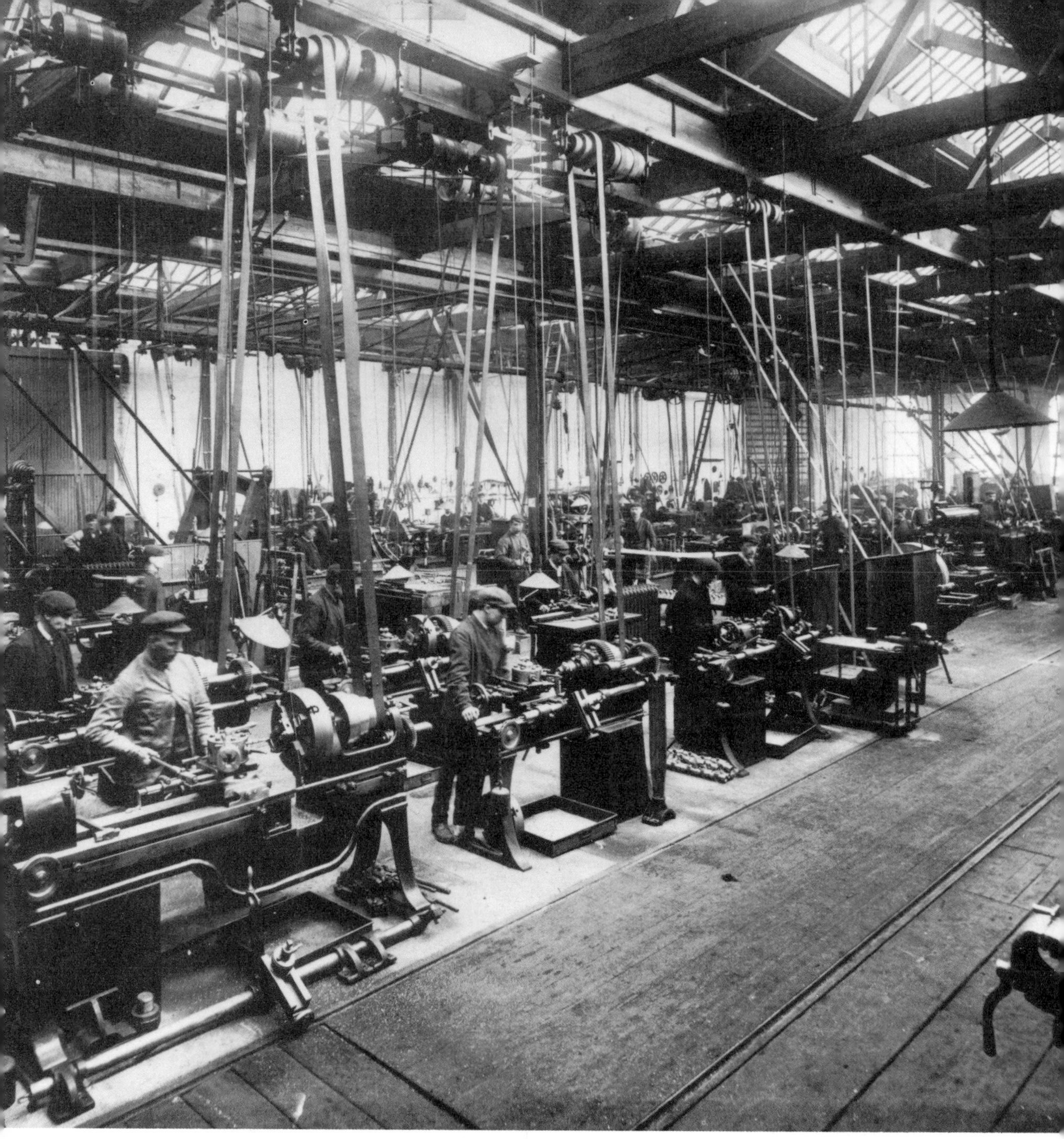

106. Keeping Glasgow's fleet of over 300 tramcars on the rails involved much engineering work. This photograph, preserved in Glasgow's Museum of Transport, shows the inside of the tramways workshop at Coplaw Road about the year 1900.

107. The nearby presence of the Lanarkshire coalfields and the existence of the mineral resources for manufacturing iron and, later, steel, resulted in the development of heavy industry in and around Glasgow. The Forge at Parkhead, photographed around 1900, had associations with Robert Napier early in the nineteenth century, but was taken over by William Beardmore, a Londoner brought up in Glasgow. He converted it into one of the greatest concerns of its kind which, by 1900, covered 49 acres.

108. The St Rollox Chemical Works were founded in 1799 by Charles Tennant, Burns's 'Wabster Charlie', and soon became the largest of their kind in Europe. This photograph was taken in 1877. Though their chimney, built in 1842, was the tallest in the world, the Works still deposited vast amounts of greyish waste over Glasgow, and were something of an eyesore.

top right **109.** Where heavy industries operated there were bound to be industrial accidents, and large firms had their own first aid squads. The North British Railways ambulance team goes through a practice in 1892.

bottom right **110.** There was work, too, for women. This girl is winding bobbins from shanks in an attic workshop in Buchanan Street in 1909.

NBR
NBR
NBR

top left **111.** Washing clothes at the entrance to the court of the Saracen's Head Inn, Gallowgate, *c.* 1902.

bottom left **112.** Farming for a time survived almost cheek by jowl with the heavy industries. Here is one such 'urban' farm, Christies, 'Blochairn', at Glenboig, where the milkmaid shown earlier was employed.

113. Modern conservationists make strenuous efforts to find new uses for older buildings. In 1897, as indeed now, not all such uses were appropriate, as is shown by this transformation of the former Free Church in Cadogan Street by Messrs. Craig and Rose, Paint and Varnish Manufacturers and Drysalters.

EASTERN BOTANIC MEDICAL HALL
CALTON WORKS
WINDOW BLIND & SUNSHADE MANUFACTORY.
JAS MEIGHAN & SON,
REGISTERED PLUMBERS, SANITARY & HEATING ENGINEERS
GAS & ELECTRIC BELL FITTERS.
ALLAN & BOGLE
BRASSFOUNDERS
CANNING STREET
61 FORREST 63
CARNIVAL
NOW OPEN
SUMMER PANTOMIME
ICE CREAM. ICE CREAM & CONFECTIONS
WM FORREST
FRY'S CHOCOLATE
OGDEN'S ROYAL NAVY "TAB" CIGARETTES
OGDEN'S GUINEA-GOLD "ROBIN REDBREAST" CIGARETTES

MILLER'S DAIRY.
DAIRY
TRY MILLER'S FINE HAND MADE BREAD
5½D. PER 4LB LOAF
5D FOR SIDES & ENDS
MILLER & SONS
LICENSED
COWFEEDERS
PEOPLE'S JOURNAL
GLASGOW GIANT
WELCOME
GRAND BALMORAL NUMBER
GIVEN GRATIS
PEOPLE'S FRIEND
FIELD MARSHAL GOUGH
INTERCEPTED LETTER

top left **114.** Nor is the jumble of self-defeating advertising entirely a new phenomenon: the east corner of Argyle Street and Canning Street in 1904.

bottom left **115.** Shops were the mainstay of life, then as now. Shop owners frequently had their premises photographed with the staff lined outside to send as Christmas cards to their customers or for other advertising purposes. Miller's Dairy, Springburn Road, in 1890.

116. The London and Glasgow Tea Company, at the corner of Kay Street and Springburn Road.

JOHN McNEILL

THE SPRINGBURN PHARMACY
ANDERSON & IRELAND,
CHEMISTS AND DRUGGISTS.
513
513

top left **117.** A butter and egg shop, owned by John McNeill. A great deal of Irish butter and quantities of eggs came to Scotland in late Victorian times, and indeed up until the 1930s, Glasgow had many Irish Butter and Egg Stores.

bottom left **118.** The Springburn pharmacy of Anderson and Ireland, *c.* 1901, with the traditional glass phials of coloured water in the shop windows.

119. When drugs were no longer of any avail, the Victorian destination was the cemetery. The Necropolis Cemetery, set up on land owned by the Merchant's House, was first used in 1832. A Lord Provost of the time is on record as saying that young people might find it inspiring to wander among the memorials to great men of the past and muse upon the brevity of human life. Many of the famous Victorian architects, including Alexander Thomson, were commissioned to provide fitting memorials to wealthy citizens who felt that their earthly success deserved ostentatious commemoration. The 1825 louring statue of John Knox, on a tall plinth, surveying his sleeping companions, is the work of sculptor Robert Forrest.